This book belongs to:

....

Author: Pip Reid

Illustrator: Thomas Barnett

Creative Director: Curtis Reid

www.biblepathwayadventures.com

Thank you for supporting Bible Pathway Adventures. Our adventure series helps parents teach their children more about the Bible in a fun creative way. Designed for the whole family, Bible Pathway Adventures' mission is to help bring discipleship back into homes around the world. The search for truth is more fun than tradition!

ISBN: 978-0-9951140-5-0

Shipwrecked!

The Adventures of Paul

"For many days neither the sun nor the stars appeared, while the storm continued to rage, until gradually all hope of survival vanished." (Acts 27:20)

A long time ago in the city Jerusalem, there lived a religious leader called Paul. Paul did not believe that Yeshua was the Messiah. He did everything he could to hurt Yeshua's followers and to put them in prison. But after God spoke to Paul on the road to Damascus, his life changed forever.

From that time on, Paul traveled from place to place, teaching the Scriptures and telling people about Yeshua.

Many religious leaders in Jerusalem did not believe Yeshua was the promised Messiah like Paul now did. They wanted Paul to stand trial for teaching lies. "Paul was one of us, and now he's speaking against our laws and traditions," they said. "We must stop him as soon as possible!"

Did you know?

Jesus' Hebrew name is Yeshua. His full name is Yehoshua, which means, 'God is my Salvation'.

To keep Paul safe from the religious leaders, a group of Roman soldiers took him to Caesarea, a city by the sea. Paul stood before Festus, the governor of Judea. "Caesar will decide if I stand trial, not these religious leaders," he said. Festus agreed with Paul. "You have appealed to Caesar, then to Caesar you go!"

Festus handed Paul and a group of prisoners over to a Roman officer named Julius. It was Julius' job to take the prisoners to Rome by ship. He stood on the deck and counted the men. One, two, three, four... "I don't want you jumping overboard and swimming away," he said.

The ship left Caesarea and sailed towards the port of Myra. Below deck, the prisoners crowded together and talked about Paul. "I heard they sent hundreds of soldiers to arrest him," one man said. "He must be a real troublemaker." The prisoners nodded their heads. Everyone in Jerusalem knew the religious leaders hated Paul because he taught people that Yeshua was the Messiah.

At the port of Myra, Julius strode up and down the wharf inspecting the ships. It was nearly wintertime and the seas were becoming rough. Julius frowned at the dark grey clouds. "I need to find a bigger ship," he said. A grain freighter would be safer and faster than the small boat they had arrived on from Caesarea.

"I have a group of soldiers and prisoners," Julius shouted up to the ships' crews. "Does anyone have room on their freighter?"

"We have space," said a captain. He hurried down the gangplank to meet Julius. Julius bought tickets for the journey and marched Paul and the prisoners onto the ship.

The captain wanted to leave Myra quickly. There were food shortages in Rome, and Caesar had offered lots of money to people who delivered grain during the dangerous winter months. "Untie the ropes," he ordered. "We're sailing to Rome!"

The ship left Myra and sailed across the sea toward Rome. But the weather soon changed and the winds began to blow harder and harder. Paul and Julius stood on the deck and stared at the sky. "I don't like the look of those clouds," said Julius.

The ship crawled through the water as slow as a snail. "This wind is too strong," the captain shouted to the sailors. "Let's sail towards the coast of Crete and find shelter from the storm."

More clouds rolled across the sky, and the winds blew even harder. No matter how hard the sailors worked they couldn't sail the ship any faster.

A few days later the ship crept into Fair Haven Harbor on the island of Crete. Paul rolled up his sleeping mat and strode over to the captain. "It's already past Yom Kippur," he warned. "If we sail on, this trip will end in disaster." The captain did not listen to Paul. "Leave it to us to sail this ship. We know what we are doing," he said.

"If we stay in the harbor, we can avoid the winter storms," argued Paul. "Why don't we leave for Rome when the seas are calm?" But captain had made up his mind to sail to Phoenix. "We can stay there for the winter if the weather is bad," he told Paul.

Paul shrugged his shoulders and sighed. He feared the captain had made the wrong decision.

Did you know?

Yom Kippur is also known as the Day of Atonement. This was the only time of the year the High Priest could enter in the Holy of Holies.

The next morning, with the wind in its sails, the ship set sail for Phoenix. The captain stood at the back of the boat, his hands on an oar. "Don't worry," he told Paul. "I've made the right decision. We'll be in Phoenix by tomorrow morning."

But as the ship sailed towards Phoenix, the winds turned into howling gales. Paul gripped the railings and watched the black clouds roll toward the ship. *"We're heading for trouble,"* he thought.

The sailors stared up at the clouds in horror. They had seen this kind of weather before. The ship was sailing into the path of a deadly storm!

Monster waves began pounding the ship. "Quick! Pull up the lifeboat and the oars," the captain commanded. The sailors dragged the lifeboat onto the deck and tied the oars to the sides. They lowered the sails from the masts and wrapped rope around the ship to hold it together.

Winds tore across the bow and waves crashed over the ship. "If the storm continues, the ship may sink," cried the captain. The sailors' hearts pounded with fear. They didn't want to drown at sea. They tied themselves to the masts and held on tight.

Did you know?

Paul was a Roman citizen.
(Acts 22:28)

The next morning, the captain made a decision. "The ship is too heavy," he shouted. "Throw the cargo overboard."

Quickly, Paul and the prisoners grabbed heavy sacks of corn and grain and dumped them into the water. "Throw the rigging overboard," yelled the sailors. They tossed the ropes and chains into the sea.

Thunder boomed overhead and lightening streaked across the sky. The ship was now at the mercy of the wind and the waves. "We're all doomed!" the sailors cried. They were too seasick to steer the ship. "We'll never make it to Rome alive!"

Paul struggled to his feet and stood in front of the shivering men. "If you had listened to me and stayed in the harbor at Crete, we wouldn't be in this mess." The men lay on the deck, clutching their stomachs. They were too sick to eat or say a word!

"Do not worry," said Paul. He turned to the captain. "A messenger from God told me I must stand before the Roman Emperor. This ship will be driven ashore onto an island, but God will save us."

The captain clung to the mast of the swaying ship and nodded his head. "I hope Paul is right," he muttered. "Anything is better than sailing through this terrible storm." He needed the sun and the stars to steer the ship, but thick black clouds covered the sky. The crew began to give up hope of ever being saved.

On the fourteenth night, the day before the Feast of Tabernacles, the men heard a strange noise. Was that the sound of waves crashing on rocks? They jumped to their feet and stared into the darkness.

A sailor tossed a measuring rope over the side to see how deep the water was. "One hundred twenty feet deep!" he yelled. A little further, he dropped the rope again. "Ninety feet deep!" The crew threw their hands in the air and cheered. They were near land. Maybe they wouldn't drown after all.

Worried the ship would smash into the rocks, the captain shouted, "Drop the anchors. We'll stay here until dawn." The sailors pushed the four anchors overboard and the ship came to a shuddering stop. The captain breathed a sigh of relief. *Phew!* His boat was safe!

A group of sailors were tired of feeling sick and wanted to go home. They came up with a clever plan. "Let's take one of the lifeboats and row ashore," they whispered to each other. They quietly lowered a lifeboat down to the water.

Paul saw what the sailors were doing and pulled Julius aside. "If those sailors escape, you have no hope of being saved," said Paul. "Tell your soldiers to stop them."

The soldiers grabbed their swords and cut the ropes to the lifeboat. "How can we escape now?" the sailors said. They sat in the lifeboat and scowled at the soldiers.

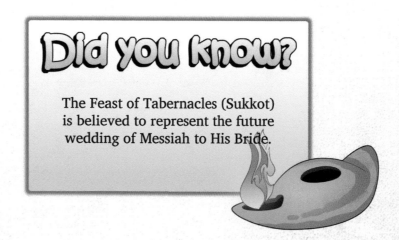

Did you know?

The Feast of Tabernacles (Sukkot) is believed to represent the future wedding of Messiah to His Bride.

Just before dawn, Paul gathered the men together on the deck. "Please eat something," he told them. "You need to stay strong. Remember that God has promised to save your lives. No one will die."

The men's stomachs grumbled loudly. Nobody had eaten for days and they were as hungry as wolves! Paul took some bread, blessed it, and began to eat.

As dawn broke, the men finally saw land. They stared silently at the sandy beach across the bay. "See that strip of sand," the captain told the sailors. He pointed to the sandy beach. "Steer the ship towards that shore."

The sailors quickly obeyed. They cut off the anchors and untied the oars, and the ship lurched forward through the crashing waves. *Crunch!* The ship crashed into a rocky reef, just as the captain had feared, and began to tear apart on the rocks. "Let's get out of here!" said the sailors. Their hearts racing with fear, they swam toward the beach as fast as they could.

"Kill the prisoners so they don't swim away and escape!" the soldiers shouted to Julius. But Julius shook his head. "No, I must save Paul's life. He must stand before Caesar in Rome."

One by one, Paul and the prisoners dived into the sea and swam across the bay to the sandy beach. They were tired of this watery adventure, and they couldn't wait to reach dry land!

Just as God had promised, everyone reached the shore safely. They had arrived on the island of Malta. The people of Malta wanted to help the men. They made a huge bonfire on the beach so the men could get warm.

Paul and the men crowded around the roaring fire, laughing and stamping their feet. They were happy to be warm and dry again. Paul was pleased to be on dry land for the Feast of Tabernacles. He quietly thanked God for saving the men's lives.

As Paul stood by the fire, a poisonous snake slithered towards him and bit him on the hand. "This man must be a murderer!" cried the locals. "He survived the shipwreck, but he won't survive this snake bite."

The people watched Paul carefully to see what would happen. But he tossed the snake into the fire without being hurt. Everyone shook their heads in amazement. "This man must be a god!" they said. "How else could he still be alive?"

Publius, the governor of Malta, gave the men a place to stay on the island. When Paul found out that Publius' father was sick, he prayed and asked God to heal the man. After this, many people came to Paul to be healed. Everyone treated him with respect and gave him many gifts.

Three months later, the captain was ready to leave for Rome. Paul hurried down to the dock and boarded the ship. He had enjoyed helping the people of Malta, but God wanted him in Rome.

It was time to stand before Caesar, the mighty Roman Emperor!

THE END

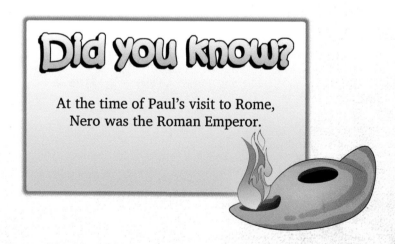

Did you know?

At the time of Paul's visit to Rome, Nero was the Roman Emperor.

TEST YOUR KNOWLEDGE!

(Match the question with the answer at the bottom of the page)

QUESTIONS

Who did Paul believe was the Messiah?

....

Why did Paul travel to Rome?

....

Who was the Roman centurion in charge of Paul?

....

Why did Paul not want to sail past Yom Kippur?

....

In which place did the captain plan to spend the winter?

....

Who tried to escape the ship in Acts 27:30?

....

Which island was Paul shipwrecked on?

....

On the island, what came out of the fire and attacked Paul?

....

How long did Paul stay on the island?

....

Whose father did Paul put his hands on and heal?

....

ANSWERS

1. Yeshua
2. To meet Caesar, the Roman emperor
3. Julius
4. Dangerous weather
5. Phoenix
6. A group of sailors
7. Malta
8. A viper (snake)
9. Approximately three months
10. Publius' father

Discover more Bible Pathway Adventures' Bible stories!

Swallowed By A Fish
Sold into Slavery
Saved by A Donkey
Thrown to The Lions
Witch of Endor
Facing the Giant
The Great Flood
The Chosen Bride
The Exodus
Escape from Egypt
Birth of the King
Betrayal of The King
The Risen King
Samson
The Temple builder

www.biblepathwayadventures.com

CPSIA information can be obtained at www.ICGtesting.com
Printed in the USA
BVIW120216310720
585128BV00012B/221

9 780995 114050